GOLF PROVERBS

GOLF METAPHORS FOR FAITH, FAMILY, AND BUSINESS

T0344625

GOLF PROVERBS

GOLF METAPHORS FOR FAITH, FAMILY, AND BUSINESS

DR. FIELD HARRISON

A SAVIO REPUBLIC BOOK
An Imprint of Post Hill Press
ISBN: 978-1-63758-210-7

Golf Proverbs:
Golf Metaphors for Faith, Family, and Business
© 2022 by Dr. Field Harrison
All Rights Reserved

Unless otherwise indicated, all Scripture quotations are taken from the Holy Bible, New Living Translation, copyright © 1996, 2004, 2015 by Tyndale House Foundation. Used by permission of Tyndale House Publishers, Carol Stream, Illinois 60188. All rights reserved.

posthillpress.com
New York • Nashville
Published in the United States of America

1 2 3 4 5 6 7 8 9 10

Introduction

Jesus always spoke in parables to His followers. In fact, he frequently used parables in combination with metaphors to teach people. His intellect and wisdom is beyond beyond, and he makes you think and figure out his meanings. "This is why I speak to them in parables: Though seeing, they do not see; though hearing, they do not hear or understand," Matthew 13:13 (NLT). Golf Proverbs was written in that same spirit, so while this is a golf book, it's also a book full of wisdom. As you read, (even this introduction) use the key, and see what He is trying to tell you. Real wisdom is never on the surface—it lies much deeper, and you have to search for it. Proverbs says, "To *fear* God is the beginning of wisdom." But Jesus commanded, "You must *love* the LORD your God with all your heart, soul, and mind." As disciples, we need to teach people that in order to love Him, we need to fear Him. Obedience is Love. This is echoed throughout the Bible. Realizing we are His and not our own is wisdom. He tests us, challenges us, and humbles us for His purpose to do His will, which is *better* than anything we could ever think, speak, or imagine. God only gives you power when you give Him power over you. If you present yourself as a living sacrifice, then He will show you heaven on earth, and give you everlasting life. That's the purpose of being His disciple.

Jesus is worth trusting, studying, leaning on, and putting your faith in because He will fight your battles, give you influence, and bless you with great friends and family. Give God what is already His and watch as miracle after miracle unfolds in your life, as it has in mine. I sincerely hope the messages in this book will light up your soul and increase your desire to learn more about God. The Bible is the most life-changing book I've read and continue to read. And don't worry, it's all good news, nothing limiting, nothing scary—only motivating you to love people and Him on another level.

metaphor | ˈmedəˌfôr | - n. a figure of speech by which one word is employed for another of which it is the image; a method of speech, or description, which likens one object to another by referring to it as if it were the other.

The Key

Golf - Jesus
Golfer - Person (**Golfers** - People)
Club - Possessions (Objects That You Own)
Play - Live
Practice - Work
Score - Success or Conquest
Shot - Task, Endeavor, or Venture
Swing - Personality
Hole - Mission, Project, or Idea
Putt - Business Deal (**Putter** - Businessman)
Course - Your Love or Lover
Game - Your Church or Business

Not every metaphor is labeled, only those most often used.

Golf - Jesus

"Fear of the Lord is the foundation of true knowledge."

Proverbs 1:7 (NLT)

Jesus came to give us life, and as golfers, golf gives us life more abundantly. Our love for golf leads us to a life-long pursuit of a relationship with the game that cannot be compared to any other. Golf is often misunderstood—but the best way to understand is to simply find a teacher.

Golf will regularly test your temper, ego, and integrity.

Golf will never apologize for disappointing you.

Only concern yourself with your own abilities in **golf**.

Never forget to thank the ones who taught you about **golf**. Even if it has been awhile.

Golf always has a way of humbling the most egotistical maniacs.

Most people who say they love **golf** are good **golfers**—but not all.

An honest loss is better than any dishonest win with **golf**.

In **golf**, love for the **game** is more important than ability.

Teaching your kids about **golf** and the traits of a good **swing** are two of the greatest gifts you can give them.

In **golf**, lacking talent should be used as motivation, not an excuse.

Golf teaches you to learn from your mistakes.

If **golf** ever becomes a chore, it's time for a **golf** lesson.

Improvement requires patience in **golf**.

Remember, **golf** should be fun.

Golf is excellent at letting you know when you're doing something wrong.

Never let anyone put a ceiling on your ability in **golf**.

The harder you try in **golf** the harder it gets.

In **golf**, remember, you can always get better.

It's not wrong to make a mistake in **golf**; it's only wrong to not admit your mistake.

Golf only rewards those who are dedicated, disciplined, and humble. Everyone else will be forgotten.

Being focused and confident are the most crucial attributes to winning in **golf**.

Keeping a **golf** journal is prudent for anyone serious about improving.

In **golf**, it's important to respect other people's habits and quirks, so they will respect yours.

Trust that your mentor knows more about **golf** than you.

Golf requires persistence, patience, and perseverance.

Golf teaches you that you will be able to **play** longer and feel better if you exercise.

Self-motivation is the only motivation that matters in **golf**.

If you take **golf** seriously, you'll get better, fast.

Who you let teach you **golf** will be the biggest decision you make in **golf**.

Talent isn't nearly as important as perseverance in **golf**.

There are a lot of secrets in **golf**; you just have to know where to look.

In **golf**, don't dwell on any mistake; just try not to make the same mistake twice.

In **golf**, being able to help those who ask for it is expected; being able to help those who never ask is a gift.

Winning is learned, not inherited, in **golf**.

If someone wants to help you in **golf**, let them.

The key to **golf** is believing in yourself.

Golf gives everyone an opportunity to be great.

Greatness is determined by how you handle your mistakes in **golf**.

Unfortunately, many people know nothing about **golf**, so be careful who you listen to.

Ensure that your success in **golf** is defined by you, and not by anyone else.

Remember, every **shot** matters in **golf**.

Other people will not stop talking just because you want them to. Animals will not be still, and birds will not stop chirping when you want them to. **Golf** teaches you to never expect this world to cater to you.

Introduce yourself to any stranger you join up with in **golf**. Friendly people have friends.

Never loan a friend a ball; just give it to him in **golf**.

Golf teaches you to be cautious by not putting the people ahead of you in any danger.

In **golf**, sometimes you're going to be partnered with people you don't like; and the only thing you can do is pray for them, be friendly, and **play**.

You will only be as good at **golf** as you think you will be.

In **golf**, when things are going good, that is when people start getting scared.

If you love **golf**, it's only a matter of time before you get good.

In **golf**, you will determine how good you get—not anyone else.

How good you get in **golf** is your responsibility; it is not anyone else's responsibility to teach you.

Golf has a way of humbling you and making you earn your **score**.

Never worry about how good someone else is at **golf**.

Golf is one of the few things you can get worse at the more you **play**.

Never quit **golf**.

Don't ever get so focused on **golf** that you forsake people.

Love for **golf** is much more important than talent in **golf**.

Golf is a beautiful teacher who loves her job.

Golfer - Person
(Golfers - People)

*"People who accept discipline
are on the pathway to life, but
those who ignore correction
will go astray."*

Proverbs 10:17 (NLT)

Becoming a good golfer takes determination, discipline, and dedication to the game. If you ignore correction, your game will suffer. You can always get better—but it is far from easy. All golfers in pursuit of improvement will share in the same sacrifice of time spent practicing—sometimes, getting worse before they get better. The process of becoming great can be slow, but it is always worth it.

Never claim to be a better **golfer** than you are.

The best **golfers** can see their mistakes before they happen, not after.

Power isn't nearly as important as most **golfers** believe.

A good **golfer** studies better **golfers** religiously.

Never brag about how good of a **golfer** you are; let other people do that.

Every accomplished **golfer** has stamina, drive, and perseverance beyond any normal human.

It's okay to be obsessed with **golf**—the best **golfers** are.

Every good **golfer** has a duty to help others learn and respect **golf**.

Ask good **golfers** lots of questions and pay attention to their answers.

Even the best **golfers** make mistakes, often.

Good **golfers** are always lucky.

A good-looking **golfers** is never as good as they look.

Many times, your **golf** coach is a worse **golfer** than you are. This doesn't mean they can't help.

The only time fear enters the heart of a bad **golfer** is when they are **playing** good.

Bad company is the ruin of good **golfers**.

The differences between being a good and great **golfer** are countless hours, unyielding focus, ability, consistency, and toughness that few people ever fully understand.

Just because you're a better **golfer** than your friend doesn't mean you're "better than" your friend.

The luckiest **golfers** are the most prepared.

Fear and fatigue are a **golfer's** two greatest enemies.

There are a lot of bad **golfers** with a lot of power.

The best **golfers practice** early in the morning.

Every **golfer** wants to improve, but very few do what it takes to improve.

Never assume someone is a bad **golfer** by the way they look.

Stretching is as necessary for a **golfer** as wearing socks.

A bad **golfer** is a potentially good **golfer** who has neither the knowledge nor experience that a good **golfer** needs to be good.

Competition brings out the best and worst in **golfers**.

A good **golfer** looks at other good **golfers** and imitates them in areas where they need improvement.

A good **golfer** doesn't need other people to tell him he's good to know that he's good.

A bad **golfer** might be brand new to the **game**, so try not to judge.

If you get an opportunity to learn from a knowledgeable **golfer**, jump at the chance.

A mediocre **golfer** is a potentially good **golfer** who simply hasn't put in the **practice** yet.

There are no shortcuts to becoming a professional **golfer**. **Practice**, **practice, practice**.

Asking someone for help is the first step to becoming a good **golfer**.

Club - Possessions
(Objects That You Own)

"Honor the Lord with your wealth and with the best part of everything you produce."

Proverbs 3:9 (NLT)

Success in golf has very little to do with equipment. Only the worst golfers will show off their clubs, while the great golfers choose to focus their attention on the form of their swings so they can score more often. In life, possessions and success don't always correlate. Success and happiness often never correlate. That is why Jesus said it is harder for a rich man to enter the Kingdom of Heaven than for a camel to enter the eye of a needle (Matthew 19:24). Though success means something different to every person, real success is most often in direct correlation to significance. Objects and possessions should help us be more significant to others, not more successful in our own eyes. If our scorecard is based on growing the Kingdom of Heaven, then we will always score.

If you throw your **clubs** on the **course**, you'll find yourself **playing** alone.

You should never grip any **club** too tight.

Clubs, by no means, make the **golfer**.

Looking at what brand of **clubs** someone else is **playing** with is pointless.

Good **players** inevitably get good **clubs**.

In order for your **swing** to generate the most power, you need to keep a light grip on every **club**.

If your grips are worn out, change your grips, not the **clubs**.

If your **clubs** are worn out, change your **clubs**, not the grips.

Good **players** don't need the best **clubs** to be good.

Used **clubs** are like used cars; they work the same, they're just cheaper and not as pretty.

Return any **club** you find.

Some of the worst **golfers** in the world have the most expensive **clubs**.

Don't ever get too attached to your **clubs**; they get stolen all the time and you should only rely on things that can't be taken away.

Nice **clubs** will only make a good **golfer** better, but a bad **golfer** would only do bad things with nice **clubs**.

Invest in good **clubs**—but first, invest in good habits; otherwise, the **clubs** will be worthless and you'll ruin them.

Remember, **clubs** do not make a good **golfer**—hard work does.

Always keep your **clubs** clean.

Play - Live

"He stores up success for the upright; He is a shield for those who live with integrity."

Proverbs 2:7 (CSB)

The way we live will deter-mine the outcome of our life, just as the way we play will determine the outcome of our game. Every human has the power to live with integrity and honor, even when the opportunity to cut corners or get ahead in a dishonorable way seems like a better option. God sees it all—and He always rewards the faithful when they play fair.

Playing your own way will be a lot harder than **playing** under the instruction of a great teacher.

Playing well under pressure is the test of a good **golfer**.

There is a big difference between **playing** and **playing** for money.

You can never be too friendly to anyone you're **playing** with.

As you **play**, take the time to look at your surroundings, and take in God's illustrious nature.

Being happy while you **play** isn't a requirement; it's a choice.

In **golf**, there will be opportunities to take risks or to **play** safe. Taking risks is more fun—but ultimately, you get to decide how you want to **play**. That's what is so great about **golf.**

You'll never **play** your best if you're watching someone else **play**.

The better you dress, the better you'll **play**.

If you're **playing** for money, every little **putt** means something.

Most people weren't meant to **play** alone, but some people prefer it.

You will **play** better around friends who are good **golfers,** than friends who are bad **golfers**.

It's always more fun to **play** by the rules in **golf**.

There are two types of people: those who love **golf** and those who watch and judge as other people **play**.

Remember, who you pick to **play** with directly impacts how well you **play**.

If you find yourself in trouble, it's time to **play** safe—or else, things could get ugly.

The older you get, the more you have to learn to **play** through the pain.

You're never too old to start **playing**.

While you **play,** mistakes are going to happen. Get over them—immediately.

You're never too old to learn the right way to **play**.

If you're **playing** with lots of money on the line, **play** safe.

You'll always **play** better after you've **practiced**.

Teaching others to **play** will remind you of things you're doing wrong.

Remember there is no need to **play** safe when there is no danger, and there is no reason to take risks for no reward.

Play within yourself.

If you're going to try to **play** safe, make sure you're **playing** safe.

Forgiveness is earned through good **playing**.

Staying angry will only make you **play** worse.

Know your limits but never **play** scared.

If you've got a good group of friends to **play** with, you should consider yourself blessed.

Keeping a level head on the **course** is a necessity if you like **playing** with others.

There are certain days you might need to **play** by yourself.

Never look for excuses as to why you're **playing** badly.

Practice - Work

"Wise words bring many benefits, and hard work brings rewards."

Proverbs 12:14 (NLT)

*I*f you want to be successful in life, you need to learn to love doing what other people hate doing. Enjoying your work is a blessing and a major key to financial success. Of course, not all aspects of work are enjoyable—but "in all labor there is profit," (Proverbs 14:23). In golf, without practice, you won't get better—but the harder you practice the more successful you'll be.

There is no substitute for **practice**.

If you're a bad **golfer** and you think things are going to magically change without **practice**, you're sadly mistaken.

If you're hurt, make sure you fully recover before you **practice** again.

Expecting to **play** well when you haven't **practiced** is like expecting to win the lottery.

Your weaknesses will never change if you never **practice** on them.

Remember, you can **practice** too much.

If you over-**practice,** your body will be the one to yell at you (along with your wife).

No matter how hard you try, you will not get better unless you **practice** the right way.

The best time to go **practice** is after a good **score**.

Some days, you will have it all figured out during **practice**, and this is not the time to take a break.

Your biggest competition is the person **practicing** harder than you.

Playing is no substitute for hard **practice**.

If you draw crowds when you **practice,** you know you're good.

Practice breeds confidence, confidence breeds success, and success breeds respect.

Consistency is earned through **practice** and patience.

Practice on what you're bad at more than what you're good at.

The only way to get better than the next guy is to out-**practice** him.

Although **practice** is the most tedious part of **golf**, it's also the most beneficial.

Remember, **practice** doesn't make perfect; perfect **practice** makes perfect.

Those who love to **practice** will be great **golfers**.

All **shots** can be mastered, it just takes **practice**.

Score - Success or Conquest

"The one who safeguards understanding finds success."

Proverbs 19:8 (HCSB)

"Success" is many things to many people—but I can promise that what God has planned for you will be greater than anything you could ever think or imagine for yourself (Ephesians 3:20). God will exceed your wildest dreams. He'll make you a leader in business, a leader in your community, a leader in your family, and will bless you more than you ever thought possible—as long as you are in His will. God created you to reflect Himself. The more you look like Him, the more He can trust you to carry out His will. But, success is the ultimate test. Power is what makes most people fail. The question is, how much success can He give you without it ruining you? Will you go after what God wants or will you go after what you want when you have the power to choose?

Golf is not about the **score**, it's about the experience.

The more honest you are with yourself and your limitations, the quicker your **score** will improve.

It's easy to lose your **score** in the sand.

Regrets will never help your **score**.

If you **play** scared, your **score** will suffer.

You earned your **score** whether you have accepted it or not.

A good **score** is dependent on an attitude of "one **shot** at a time."

The least important attribute of scoring in **golf** is power.

There is a direct correlation between how hard you worked and how low you **scored**.

Don't let your **score** prevent you from having fun.

You always deserve your **score**.

There is only one way to lower your blood pressure, increase stamina, and improve your **score**: by walking.

Your **score** will be decided by how well you **play** through your worst **hole**, not your best.

Nothing will improve your **score** faster than a mentor.

If your mind is anywhere else, your **score** will suffer.

When your **score** is looking good, remember to stay calm—do not change your strategy or get too excited.

In **scoring** low, confidence is your most deadly mannerism.

Putting too much pressure on yourself will result in a worse **score**.

One low **score** is nice, but consistency requires **practice**.

Never get upset at a **score**, just learn from your mistakes.

Remember, the only person who cares about your **score** is you.

Never forget that par is always a good **score.**

Your **score** will be decided before you walk up to the first tee, based on your preparation.

The path to **scoring** is long, fun, and worth every second.

Whether you're aware of your **score** or not, make sure you focus on the **hole** you're on.

Shot - Task, Endeavor, or Venture

"Commit your actions to the Lord, and your plans will succeed."

Proverbs 16:3 (NLT)

*E*very shot you take in life includes the potential for risk and reward. The same goes with golf—the better you know yourself and where you make mistakes, the more you can actively avoid them on the course, and the better your game will be. You need to know your strengths and weaknesses to succeed in both golf and life. Every shot you take in life makes God proud because you cannot take a shot without faith. Every shot and every effort to an endeavor makes God smile because it's an act of faith. I pray you see reward in every shot you take.

With every **shot**, listen to your eyes but only trust your gut.

Every **shot** in **golf** is a learning experience.

Many people mistakenly think some **shots** are difficult when they're not, and other **shots** are easy when they're not.

Aim on every **shot**.

With every **shot**, have an order by which you do things and be consistent.

Don't let other people distract you from your next **shot**.

Every **shot** has repercussions.

Difficult **shots** only reward skilled **golfers**.

Remember to aim for something specific on every **shot**.

Unfortunately, every bad **shot** is usually coupled with another bad **shot**.

Every **shot** needs to account for both your strengths and weaknesses.

If you're going to **play** safe, make sure your **shot** is safe; unfortunately, this can be extremely difficult to judge.

Give yourself room to make mistakes with every **shot**.

Many good **shots** end up in the hazard area.

Overestimating **shots** is equally as harmful as underestimating **shots** in **golf**.

Meticulous preparation is mandatory for the success of each **shot**.

On any **shot**, being short and safe is better than being long and in trouble.

Never take an easy **shot** for granted.

Get over bad **shots** immediately.

Remember, if your **shot** finds trouble, **golf** is teaching you something.

Fatigue makes easy **shots** hard.

Always think about how this **shot** will affect the next **shot**, and plan accordingly.

With every **shot**, make sure you know where you might miss it.

Only take a chance on a **shot** after you've calculated all the risks.

With every **shot**, your ball will always follow your feet.

Swing - Personality

"The spirit of man is the lamp of the Lord, searching and examining all the innermost parts of his being."

Proverbs 20:27 (AM)

 golfer's swing might be the most important aspect of their game, just as love is the most important attribute of Christianity. We are commanded by Jesus to love both God and people (Matthew 22:36–40). Obeying these two commands is fundamental to having life more abundantly. Love is what sets us apart as light in the darkness. Whoever loves the most is the most powerful person in any room. Just as a golfer needs to practice the form of their swing, Christians need to practice being more loving, more generous, more kind, more patient, more gentle, and more self-controlled in all aspects of life. Just as a golfer can spot a pro by their swing, people can spot a believer by their ability to love.

Having a smooth **swing** has many advantages.

In each **swing**, the older the habit, the harder it is to fix.

Your **swing** will be as consistent as your routine.

Just because you expect others to be silent while you show off your **swing** doesn't mean they will.

You'll only go as far in **golf** as your **swing** takes you.

It's always people with bad **swings** that are the first to correct other people's **swings**.

If your **swing** is bad, your body will unfortunately remind you.

Make sure your **swing** always follows through.

Pressure can make even the best **golfers swing** bad.

Bad **golfers** never change their **swing**.

Remember, you will never have complete control over the **shot** no matter how good your **swing** is.

A **swing** is just one aspect of their **game**; don't assume anything until you've seen them **play**.

When most people see their **swing** on video, they are shocked at what they see (it's a great teaching device).

A great **swing** seems effortless, but it took relentless determination to become that way.

Every **swing** change will be very uncomfortable at the beginning; that's just the nature of change.

Power is generated in every aspect of the **swing**, not just one phase.

It's expected for your **swing** to change with different **clubs**.

The brain remembers everything in a **swing**—both good and bad habits.

A good **swing** is always striving to get better.

Just because a perfect **swing** is unattainable doesn't mean you should stop trying.

Trust your **swing**.

Every **swing** can be improved.

One good **swing** may look nothing like another good **swing**, but they keep the same fundamentals.

A good **swing** is a beautiful thing to see and hear.

There are an infinite number of unique, incredible **swings**.

A bad **swing** is only as bad as the end result.

Some **golfers** have **swings** that people assume are "bad" or "different," but actually, they're very good.

No two **swings** are the same.

If you think you have a problem with your **swing**, you're probably right.

If your **swing** makes you hurt, you need to see a professional for help.

If you've developed a bad habit with your **swing**, stop and fix it immediately—otherwise, it just becomes more arduous to overcome later.

The best **golfers** optimize confidence, power, consistency, rhythm, and timing in the **swing**.

Hole - Mission, Project, or Idea

"Let your eyes look straight ahead; fix your gaze directly before you."

Proverbs 4:25 (NIV)

In life, your most important mission is discovering your calling and living it out. You can be called more than once. You can love more than once. You can succeed more than once—and you will fail more than once in your pursuit of success. But no mission is worth depression. No hole is deserving of an overreaction. Mistakes and failures will inevitably happen, but God promises to be with us through it all (Hebrews 13:5). God calls us to overcome every obstacle just as His Son, Jesus, overcame everything for us. Don't quit because of difficult rounds—play well, practice hard, and you will eventually score.

Never give up on any **hole**.

Not being an idiot will save you countless **shots** on any **hole**.

Tough **holes** need preparation.

Never blow the **hole** on a one-footer.

Each **hole**, you have one goal—to score.

Every **hole** needs a plan, and a back-up plan— and it probably won't go as either planned.

Not every **hole** is fun.

If the group ahead of you is taking a long time on the **hole**, take your time.

Never blow the **hole** on an easy **shot**.

There are going to be **holes** that just have your number; on these, **play** safe.

Remain indifferent to your competition in both their good and bad **holes**.

One bad **hole** can cost you the competition.

Remember, the first **shot** is the most important **shot** of every **hole**.

Finish every **hole**—unless you're a beginner.

Strategy becomes much more important with the hard **holes**.

The difference between winning and losing is usually determined by how well you did on your worst **holes**, not your best.

Manage every **hole** the easiest way.

Nobody cares how talented someone is if they can't keep the pace on every **hole**.

Every **hole** needs a plan, and every plan needs preparation.

Realize you may do everything right and still bogey the **hole**.

Every **hole** has its secrets—figure them out.

Every **hole** has areas of danger—avoid these areas.

Some **holes** are so hard, bogey is a good **score**.

Always use a tee on every **hole**.

Putt - Business Deal
(Putter - Businessman)

"Do you see any truly competent workers? They will serve kings rather than working for ordinary people."

Proverbs 22:29 (NLT)

*I*f you want a successful business, surround yourself with amazing people. A good team is a miracle to pray for because they will allow you to succeed the fastest and to endure the longest through every season your business will go through. If someone lies or cheats in one aspect of their life, then you can know that they will lie and cheat in every aspect of their lives. Look for godly character and integrity in your relationships. The people you choose to partner with will affect every aspect of your life, business, marriage, and personal friendships. Both putting in golf and partnerships in business take a great deal of patience and alignment. Choose the people you play with wisely.

Every good **putter** has their own style and routine—make your own.

There are many different ways to make a **putt**.

Make sure your grip isn't too tight or too loose on important **putts**.

Sometimes your **game** can be lost on one **putt**.

Remember, you can get too confident with a **putt**.

Just because you made a big **putt** doesn't mean everyone's going to be happy for you.

Never second guess your approach—fully commit to the **putt**.

Sometimes a **putt** looks like it's going to go one way, and it turns in a totally different direction.

Sometimes your worst **putt** is your best **putt**.

Look at each **putt** from every angle.

Whether you're a good **putter** or a bad **putter**, you have to believe you're a great **putter**.

Remember, not every **putt** is made.

Always try to leave yourself a "tap in" with every **putt**.

Long **putts** require feel and aim—and luck.

The speed of a **putt** always takes precedence over everything.

Always try to make every **putt**.

Remember, a lot can go wrong on an easy **putt**.

Being nervous will only hurt your **putts**.

All **putts** require a keen sense of feel.

Pay close attention to detail with every **putt**.

Start assessing the situation as soon as you start walking up on a **putt**.

Never lose your cool for missing an easy **putt**.

Never accept missing any **putt** you shouldn't have.

Never rush a short, easy **putt** and you'll never have to forgive yourself for blowing it.

Have a routine and stick with it for every **putt**.

If you make the **putts** you should make and miss the **putts** you shouldn't make, you should have no complaints.

Short, easy **putt** are the **shots** you can control—always be firm on a **shot** you can control.

If you're missing every **putt**, make sure your eyes are over the ball.

There is nothing that can change your momentum like making a big **putt**.

If you can't read the **putt**, look at the **putt** from a different perspective.

All good **putters** can see the path the **putt** will take the entire length of the **putt**.

Every **putt** is missable.

Every **putt** is makeable.

Course - Your Love or Lover

"Whoever pursues righteousness and unfailing love will find life, righteousness, and honor."

Proverbs 21:21 (NLT)

Who and what you love will determine the course of your life. If you fall in love with a God-fearing, God-loving person, then you will find that favor and blessing will continually chase you down. If you treat your lover wrongly, then what could God ever trust you with? Much of this life is a test of how strong, forgiving, patient, and true your love really is. Is your love reflective of His love? This test is the hardest test of life and I pray you get to love and be loved as you guard your heart above all things. To all the broken hearts, I pray for a full heart recovery, so your heart will heal, and you will love and trust again in Jesus' name.

Leave the **course** prettier than you found it.

You might notice that if you're away from the **course** too long, you get depressed. That's normal.

Some days will be better than others on the **course**.

Never gamble on a **course** you don't know.

Never blame the **course** for your mistakes.

Most people get mad at the **course** when *they* are **playing** badly.

The **course** is as close as you'll ever get to the Garden of Eden.

Respect the **course**; fix every scar, whether you made it or not.

If your son is watching you throw a temper tantrum on the **course**, chances are, he will too.

No **course** is perfect, but every **course** is beautiful.

Even if the **course** makes you want to scream, try your hardest not to.

If someone is going to cheat on the **course**, they are going to cheat on everything.

The smell of a **course** never gets old.

Make it your responsibility to make sure others treat the **course** respectfully.

Every **course** becomes more difficult if you're **playing** badly.

The **course** that challenges you will be the easiest to love.

There's never been a **golfer** who couldn't smile at a **course**.

The **course** will require your full attention if you have any intention of **scoring**.

Just because you had some alcohol is no excuse for losing your mind on the **course**.

Just because you love the **course** doesn't mean the **course** is going to be nice.

Every **course** has a story—all you have to do is ask.

The **course** is always changing in little ways, but big changes take time.

The hardest parts of a **course** never change.

If you don't know the **course**, you can never expect to **play** mistake-free.

Anyone who has ever been on a **course** knows its power.

The more manicured and decorated **courses** are, the more expensive and difficult they become.

Never get angry or sulky on the **course**—no one on a **course** has any room to complain.

If the **course** isn't heaven, it's as close as we are ever going to get.

Some of the prettiest **courses** will give you the most trouble.

The **course** is always changing, slowly with time— just like you.

Certain parts of the **course** are always prudent to avoid.

If you're cheating on a **course**, you're only cheating yourself.

Patience is a necessity on the **course**.

Never forget that the best **course** in the world was made just for you.

If the **course** can't make you smile, nothing will.

Game - Church or Business

"The name of the Lord is a strong fortress; the godly run to Him and are safe."

Proverbs 18:10 (NLT)

When you live according to godly principles, your life will benefit—just as when you play according to the rules of golf, the success of your game will increase. Jesus came to give us life and life more abundantly (John 10:10), and that promise is for everyone willing to give up their life for Him. As we devote our gifts and talents to grow God's Kingdom on earth, our calling and purpose collide.

Honor the **game** and dress appropriately.

Although your bad friends might be more fun to **play** with, your **game** will pay the price.

Sharing your philosophies about the **game** with your kids will never get old.

If someone doesn't share your opinions or philosophies about the **game,** it's okay. Not everyone has to agree.

In **golf**, you're the team; there is no one to blame for your **game** but you.

No matter how good your **game** is, you're still going to have bad days.

A good **golfer** only focuses on his own **game** and doesn't worry about anyone else's **game**.

One of the best things about **golf** is, even if you've lost your **game**, you can always get it back.

Your **game** will suffer if you don't **practice** it.

If you're drinking in excess, more than just your **game** will suffer.

A **golfer's game** is brought down by cheating, cursing, and drinking.

When your **shot** ends up in trouble, your **game** will be the most scrutinized. How will you recover?

Weekly lessons will keep your **game** on track; but if it has been a while, you might have gotten good at doing the wrong thing.

Just because they have a good **swing** doesn't mean they have a good **game**. A good **swing** may be all they have.

Be aware that work, friends, kids, and significant others can distract you from the **game**—it happens to the best of **golfers** every so often.

If you're a good **golfer**, your **game** will prove it.

Your **game** is your responsibility.

If you have a bad temper, it's your **game** that pays the price, no one else's.

You have no right to judge anyone else's **game**.

Be true to your **game**.

Nobody's **game** is perfect but being able to scramble out of trouble is the key to **scoring**.

Your **game** will suffer if any aspect of your **game** is ignored.

When someone spends money and time on their **game**, they're on track to being a good **golfer**.

You're never going to **play** mistake-free—that's just part of the **game**.

New **clubs** will usually do nothing for your **game**.

The hardest **shots** to master in the **game** are the most beneficial.

Never consider quitting the **game** due to any mistake, bad experience, or lack of progress. Getting good at **golf** takes time, experience, and mistakes.

Your **game** is only as important as you prioritize it to be.

Don't let any mistake ruin your **game**.

A Note from the Author

I am humbled to have been called to write this book and I hope it inspires a deeper pursuit into His word and His purpose for all readers. Our highest calling is His calling for us, and I am convinced this book was His doing.

As I started writing a book about golf, God took over and it started becoming something entirely different—a spiritual metaphor book. Due to some keen insights from my brilliant book agent, Jan Miller (who is a genius), it turned out to be a much better book than I could have ever anticipated, and I am so thankful for the astute observations she brought to this project.

I also want to thank the best Mom and Dad in the world for giving me a rock of confidence by their unwavering commitment to one another and their constant support for me. I love you both more than words can say.

I want to thank my pastor (and friend) Bishop T.D. Jakes, for teaching, inspiring, and praying for me. I, along with everyone who knows you, see Jesus in you.

I also want to thank Pastors Jim and Becky Hennesy for believing and investing in me. You both love people so much that they can't help but follow you as you follow Jesus.

And to all my supporting friends, I am so thankful for each of you. You all have inspired and taught me so much, and I hope you all know how much I love you.

I want to thank Amy Noelck, for her patience and kindness in being my writing mentor.

I want to thank my Grammie for introducing me to the game of golf. I love you.

I want to thank my soulmate and my closest friend, my moon and my stars—my beautiful wife, Sabrina. For all you do and for all you are, I will love you forever.

I want to thank my kids, Field Christian and Camila—you both have taught me more about God than anyone.

And finally, thank you God for giving me such wonderful people in my life. I am forever grateful.

—Dr. Field Harrison

About the Author

D r. Field Harrison is the co-founder of AMEN Church at the world-renowned Meyerson Symphony Center in downtown Dallas, Texas. He is also the founder of MINT dentistry, one of the fastest-growing firms in America. While an author, speaker, entrepreneur, and dentist by trade—above all, Dr. Harrison is a messenger for Christ and a devoted husband to his beautiful wife, Sabrina, and a proud dad to two incredible children named Field Christian and Camila. He is passionate about God, dentistry, golf, and giving back to his community. Since founding MINT dentistry in 2009, Dr. Harrison has used his business as a platform to financially support many local churches and has given to many other philanthropic endeavors. Dr. Harrison also privately assists MINT employees who are experiencing financial hardship through his internal charitable organization known as MINT Cares.